Dedication

This book is dedicated to the Glory of God,
through His Son, Jesus Christ.

Acknowledgements

First and foremost, I want to thank my God for everything. He is the Reason I am here today.

Thank you to my husband Greg, my friend and soul-mate. I love you more than you know.

To my children Sam, Jacob, Ellison and Laura – I love each of you tremendously. You put the sparkle in my shine.

To my mom, Allen, Debbie, Tim, Mama B, Pop, Elizabeth, Shiela, Robyn – thank you all for your love and encouragement. There are others too numerous to name.

To my church families in Gastonia and Leland – you Shine with His light.

To the children of Zambia, Africa – I left a part of my heart there. I'll be back one day to see it.

This book is in memory of my dad, John Bentley, and a little boy named Braxton.

Unto Us a Child is Born

Terrie Bentley McKee

Set Time

In the beginning, immediately after the Original Sin occurred in the Garden of Eden, God set in motion the only Way for humanity to be wiped clean: "And I will put enmity between you and the woman, and between your offspring and hers; he will crush your head, and you will strike his heel," [Genesis 3:15].

This longing for a Messiah stretched over hundreds of years. The Old Testament, which was written over a thousand-year period, contains 353 prophecies about the coming Messiah. Some prophecies focus on His death, others on His Second Coming. There are about 10 or so prophecies that were fulfilled at His birth.

High priests, scribes, the religious elite, and all men who listened to teachings in the temple knew that God was going to bring a Ruler, a King, to rule over His own. They knew that this King would be born of a virgin in Bethlehem:

"For to us a child is born,

to us a son is given,
and the government will be on his shoulders.
And he will be called
Wonderful Counselor, Mighty God,
Everlasting Father, Prince of Peace."
~ Isaiah 9:6

"Therefore the Lord himself will give you a sign:
The virgin will conceive and give birth to a son,
and will call him Immanuel."
~ Isaiah7:14

"But you, Bethlehem Ephrathah,
though you are small among the clans of Judah,
out of you will come for me
one who will be ruler over Israel,
whose origins are from of old,
from ancient times." ~ Micah 5:2

As the Roman Empire conquered the Holy Land
and increased its grip on Israel, people prayed
and hoped for an earthly king, to rid the land of
the Roman governors, the roadside crucifixions,
the ever-present Roman legions.

As time marched on, and God did not bring forth
the Messiah when the people thought He would,
prophets became fewer and fewer in number. As

Malachi wraps up his book with the promise, "I will send my messenger, who will prepare the way before me. Then suddenly the Lord you are seeking will come to his temple; the messenger of the covenant, whom you desire, will come," says the Lord Almighty." [Malachi 3:1], the Old Testament ends, starting a period between the Old and New Testaments in which God is incredibly, painfully silent.

Have you ever experienced a time in which you were praying for something -- perhaps an answer for a new job, or for a loved one to be healed. Perhaps you were looking for healing — healing of your marriage, your body, your church ... and God was incredibly quiet. There is a choice to be made here: either you lack faith, stop praying, and draw farther away from God, or the opposite. You dig into the Scriptures and continue praying, despite the oppressive quiet. You claim the promise that God hears us, as John wrote: "This is the confidence we have in approaching God: that if we ask anything according to his will, he hears us," [1 John 5:14]. We must claim the confidence we have in our Risen Lord that He hears us — despite all evidence to the contrary.

For 400 long years between the time the Old

Testament ended and the New Testament dawned, God was quiet — but working. God works in His timing — not ours. Habakkuk wrote, "For the revelation awaits an appointed time; it speaks of the end and will not prove false. Though it linger, wait for it; it will certainly come and will not delay." Titus wrote, "And which now at his appointed season he has brought to light through the preaching entrusted to me by the command of God our Savior," [1:3].

Did you catch that? "Awaits an appointed time" and "At HIS appointed season...." God, in His divine glory, is in charge of time, not the other way around. He knew, while He was even standing before Adam, Eve and the serpent in the Garden, *exactly* when His Son would come onto the earthly scene. He had a set time planned and put into motion of His own creation and working when a young girl named Mary would be born. It did not catch God by surprise that a young carpenter named Joseph would be interested in Mary as his bride — for God ordained it.

Look at Galatians 4:4: "But when the set time had fully come, God sent his Son, born of a woman, born under the law." When the set time had fully come....The time had nothing to do with our, human, timing. It had everything to do with God's timing.

We have the benefit of the Scriptures as a rear-view mirror of sorts to see how prophecies were fulfilled. Luke wrote, "Many have undertaken to draw up an account of the things that have been fulfilled among us, just as they were handed down to us by those who from the first were eyewitnesses and servants of the word. With this in mind, since I myself have carefully investigated everything from the beginning, I too decided to write an orderly account for you, most excellent Theophilus, so that you may know the certainty of the things you have been taught," [1:1-4]. We have Luke's detailed, physicians' eye to bring to life the Christmas story.

We have eyewitness accounts of how God fulfilled prophecies, answered prayers, and gave to us the promise of His timing. Let us remember that the God Who set the appointed time for His Son, is the same God Who sets the time of His Son's return, and answers prayers for His people.

For Reflection:

Read Psalm 40:1. When was a time that you waited patiently for the Lord? When was a time you waited impatiently for Him?

What were any differences in your feelings between the two times?

How can you slow down the often crazy-busy Christmas season to positively reflect on God's gift to us in His Son?

After David died, his son and heir to the throne, Solomon, found that there were so many priests that it became necessary to divide and delegate responsibilities. First Chronicles 24:10 and 19 mentions one such priestly division. "...The seventh to Hakkoz, the eighth to Abijah," [verse 10]. This meant, that all the men who belonged to the priestly division of Hakkoz were seventh in line to serve in the temple, and Abijah was eighth in line.

This is important, as the Lord laid out this plan that Abijah specifically would be eighth in line to serve in the temple, as 1 Chronicles 24:19 states: "This was their appointed order of ministering when they entered the temple of the Lord, according to the regulations prescribed for them by their ancestor Aaron, as the Lord, the God of Israel, had commanded him." But why is this important?

The division of Abijah was eighth in line to serve in the temple. For the men in the divisions, who were chosen by lot to burn incense in the Holy of Holies, this was literally a once-in-a-lifetime event, as a man could only serve God in such a supremely honorable way once in his life. Enter a righteous and devote man named Zechariah, married to Elizabeth, who was belonged to the division of Abijah and was chosen to light the incense.

Indeed, Zechariah must have been experiencing mixed emotions as he slowly ascended up the stairs to the temple: elation and honor at such an incredible moment in his life, and, at the same time, embarrassment and concern for his wife who was barren. For a Jewish couple, not having children was a stigma that was never removed, even in their old age. Yet, Zechariah and Elizabeth were righteous "in the sight of God," [v. 6]. Perhaps Zechariah thought that after the prescribed prayers he would recite, he would take this opportunity to call upon the Name of the Lord on behalf of his wife's empty womb.

As he lit the incense, no doubt hearing the worshipers' prayers from outside, suddenly, Zechariah was not alone. Gabriel the mighty archangel delivered his customary "do not fear" statement with a solid answer to Zechariah's personal petitions: "Do not be afraid, Zechariah; your prayer has been heard. Your wife Elizabeth will bear you a son, and you are to call him John. He will be a joy and delight to you, and many will rejoice because of his birth, for he will be great in the sight of the Lord. He is never to take wine or other fermented drink, and he will be filled with the Holy Spirit even before he is born. He will bring back many of the people of Israel to the Lord their God. And he will go on before the Lord, in the spirit and power of Elijah, to turn the hearts of the parents to their children and the disobedient to the wisdom of the righteous — to make ready a people prepared for the Lord," [Luke 1:13-17].

Perhaps it was complete shock at visually seeing an archangel, or the news that Elizabeth would bear a child, let alone a son who would be destined to be the forerunner of the Messiah — perhaps it was the thought that the boy, John, would be patterned after the great Elijah...at any rate, one can almost hear Zechariah's words stumble out of his mouth wondering how he could be sure of this. Gabriel tells Zechariah that because of his unbelief, he would be mute — until the "appointed time" [v. 20].

Yes, Zechariah was chosen by chance to serve, but it was anything but a random occurrence. God knew the players, scenes and sets....He wrote the play! He knew, way back, that the division of Abijah would be serving at this time, that Zechariah would be part of that house, and He orchestrated the lot to fall to Zechariah. In this grand plan to bring John into the world to be the forerunner of Christ, there is nothing here that "just happened." Circumstances did not land Zechariah before the incense in the Holy of Holies — God-stance did.

The phrase "appointed time" rings throughout this story that is tucked in at the very beginning of Luke, just a few chapters away from when the very-busy Gabriel made another unexpected call on a young girl in Nazareth. God appoints these moments of history in His plan and His timing. He knew that a descendant of Abijah's would be this elderly, childless priest. He knew that if John's parents had not been childless, they would not have worshiped and been in awe of the blessings of God through their son. God closed Elizabeth's womb until He decided it would be opened — at the appointed time.

It brings new meaning to God's words to

Jeremiah: "For I know the plans I have for you," declares the Lord, "plans to prosper you and not to harm you, plans to give you hope and a future. Then you will call on me and come and pray to me, and I will listen to you. You will seek me and find me when you seek me with all your heart," [Jeremiah 29:11-13].

For Reflection…

Looking back on your life, what times can you remember were obviously orchestrated by God? How do you know?

Zechariah's entire family line seemed to lead up to the moment that he served in the temple. Have there been times in your life that seemed lead up to a particular event or situation?

What are you waiting on right this minute? What prayer request is always on your lips? Present this petition before the Lord and know that yes, He does hear it. Ask Him for patience and faith to wait for His timing and for His will to be done.

God's Favor

It is incredible and wonderful that God chose to mark time of His Son's earthcoming using an elderly woman's pregnancy: "In the sixth month of Elizabeth's pregnancy, God sent the angel Gabriel to Nazareth, a town in Galilee, to a virgin pledged to be married to a man named Joseph, a descendant of David. The virgin's name was Mary. The angel went to her and said, "Greetings, you who are highly favored! The Lord is with you," [Luke 1:26-28].

It is equally incredible and wonderful that Gabriel addressed young Mary, whom biblical scholars estimate to be about 12 years old, as "you who are highly favored." Mary joined the ranks of Abel, who had God's favor because he righteously chose the first fruits of his flock, and of Noah, who had God's favor because he righteously walked with God even in the midst of a storm of sin around him. Mary, a young woman, engaged to a righteous man named Joseph — both of whom were descendants of David, who also had God's favor.

Mary, with the mighty archangel Gabriel standing before her, was "troubled" at his words, Scripture said, even going so far as stating that Mary "wondered what kind of greeting this might be," [v. 29].

God shows up in our lives and we wonder what in the world is He up to? In 2012, I prayed that God would allow me to go on a mission trip. I was thinking the Appalachian mountains, Florida, or somewhere else that was a day's drive away. Then, to my shock and awe, God revealed rather suddenly, "Africa." Africa is most decidedly not a day's drive away...I wondered very much what kind of greeting that was, when God very clearly said "Africa" — then proceeded to provide the funds for the journey, which occurred in September-October 2013. That African mission trip changed my life, blessings upon blessings, and I give all the glory to God for the 45 children who accepted Christ as their Savior in the village where we served.

Mary, though, was about to embark on a once-in-humanity adventure, as Gabriel explained to her, "You will conceive and give birth to a son, and you are to call him Jesus. He will be great and will be called the Son of the Most High. The Lord God will give him the throne of his father David, and he will reign over Jacob's descendants forever; his kingdom will never end," [v. 31-33].

As she stood there, the thoughts through her head must have been like a waterfall of emotions... Conceive. Virgin. Son.

Jesus.

The Messiah whom she had heard about all her life, the Savior of her nation, this Wonderful, Counselor, Almighty God, Prince of Peace....she was to conceive and bear this Child, and give Him the name Jesus. *Jesus.* A thousand years' longing for the Messiah and finally His Name crosses angelic lips and into the ears of the first human to hear His name, and it's His mother's ears who hears her Savior's name first...*Jesus.*

Mary then gathers her courage and showcases the righteousness and faith that made God smile upon her: "How will this be," Mary asked the angel, "since I am a virgin?"

This question was not like Zechariah's question, "How can I be sure of this? I am an old man and my wife is well along in years." His question asked for proof; Mary's question was one of logistics, since she was not just a virgin, but an engaged virgin.

Mary knew the Law and the ramifications of a pregnancy out of wedlock. Yet, she trusted God. Everything that was taught to her about the Law seemed to scream against this, but what could she do? She, Mary, was highly favored by the Lord God of Hosts, Who made the Law.

"I am the Lord's servant," Mary answered. "May your word to me be fulfilled." She humbled herself, answered in the words and tone of a servant, and accepted the Word as fulfilled to her.

And God smiled.

For Reflection...

Describe a time in your life in which you committed whole-heartily, without question, to God's call.

How was this time different than times in which you fought His call upon your life?

Joy

Joy to the World! We hear that Christmas carol in stores, on the radio, at churches, but do we hear it in our hearts this Christmas season?

We get so caught up in the stuff of Christmas that we don't pay much attention to the simplicity of Christmas. Parties, presents, decorations, cookies, gingerbread houses, lights, obligatory fruitcake....Christmas has become a distraction that fuels depression more than anything. Yet, the joy of Christmas started when a young pregnant virgin visited her elderly pregnant cousin and called out her name, "Elizabeth!"

"When Elizabeth heard Mary's greeting, the baby leaped in her womb, and Elizabeth was filled with the Holy Spirit....As soon as the sound of your greeting reached my ears, the baby in my womb leaped for joy," [Luke 1:41, 44].

The prenatal John the Baptist heard Mary's greeting and did a somersault in joy as his mother was filled with the Holy Spirit. Do we still feel that way about Christmas? Or have we become so jaded by the tinsel and toil that we forget just how simple Christmas is?

Do we still feel the same way about *Jesus*? For it is truly as simple as this complex thought:

"For God so loved the world that he gave his one and only Son, that whoever believes in him shall not perish but have eternal life," [John 3:16].

We need to re-connect with the joy of Christmas, which is not found in any store, or at any party, or in a gingerbread house. It is found simply in our hearts — if — and only if — Jesus has already taken up residence through accepting Him as Savior. Salvation through Jesus Christ is the only way to truly have the joy of Christmas, for it is then that we experience this incredible fact: Only Jesus can sand off the rough-hewn boards of our own mangers, covered in sin, and make something incredible: new creations, fit for His service, with joy in our hearts.

Christmas joy is anchored in salvation. He came to this earth as a helpless baby to grow up and die for us, just so we can be reconciled back to the Father. How can we not have joy in our souls knowing that Jesus has washed us, whiter than snow, and made us free from sin? How can we not have joy in our salvation knowing that Jesus knows our names and has written them in His Book of Life?

How can we sing songs of praise to God our Father about Him while frowning or not singing out with our whole heart?

"Come," wrote the psalmist in Psalm 95:1, "Let us sing for joy to the Lord; let us shout aloud to the Rock of our salvation."

Christmas joy is joy unhindered, that should make us want to do somersaults and cartwheels and praise God from the highest rooftops! Jesus, Immanuel, God with us! Jesus, Prince of Peace, here to give us peace! Jesus, Savior, Light of the world! *Joy!*

For Reflection:

Reflect on Luke 1:46-56. Write down everything Mary said God has done.

Now, write down everything God has done in your life. Reflect on the current status of joy in your life, and if you need to, pray that God will give you the joy of your salvation.

When is it hard to praise God? During difficulties, sorrow or pain? Pray to Him, and ask Him to reveal Himself to you in tangible ways, and praise Him for each way He shows that He is with you.

He Didn't Stay in the Manger

I have a Nativity set that has been in my family
for over 60 years. It has been out with the other
Christmas decorations as long as I can remember.
Now, it graces my home, on a built-in shelf in my
living room. It's plastic, and to be honest, is made
up of garish colors straight from the bowels of
1954. It is nonetheless a beloved piece of our
Christmas decor. Each time I walk past it or look
at it I notice, though, that baby Jesus has slipped
out of the manger and is resting on the shelf.

I put the plastic figurine back in the manger.

He slips back out.

Over and over, all through the Christmas season,
I have placed the baby back in the manger. He
slips back out again. I was about to get out the
hot glue gun and get the Baby Jesus to stay in
there, but then I had this incredible, amazing
thought:

He didn't stay in the manger.

Think about it: the *real* Baby Jesus didn't stay a baby, and didn't stay in the manger. The Bible says that His mother and adopted father Joseph took him, eight days old, directly to the Temple as devout Jewish parents did in those times.

While there, they were greeted by old Simeon, who was filled with the Holy Spirit. "Simeon took him in his arms and praised God, saying: "Sovereign Lord, as you have promised, you may now dismiss your servant in peace. For my eyes have seen your salvation, which you have prepared in the sight of all nations: a light for revelation to the Gentiles, and the glory of your people Israel," Luke 2:28-32.

For my eyes have seen your salvation! Simeon hit the nail on the head. Jesus came on a mission, and even as a little eight-day-old newborn, had the Spirit of God resting on Him so that an aged man, who had been waiting on the Lord day and night, rejoiced with Jesus in his arms.

Jesus didn't stay in the line of people and family coming back from Passover in Jerusalem. Joseph and Mary looked for Him for three days — *three days!* Then, there He was — in the Temple, teaching the elders! I bet Mary and Joseph didn't know whether to be proud or embarrassed. "Why were you searching for me?" he asked. "Didn't you know I had to be in my Father's house?" [Luke 2:49]

Luke writes here that Jesus didn't stay a precocious twelve year old. Jesus "grew in wisdom and stature, and in favor with God and man," [2:52].

Jesus' whole purpose was to preach the Good News of His coming, and for salvation — to die a sinner's death on a cross. "He has saved us and called us to a holy life — not because of anything we have done but because of his own purpose and grace. This grace was given us in Christ Jesus before the beginning of time, [2 Timothy 1:9].

Jesus sacrificed Himself on the cross, willingly laying His life down for us. He willed Himself to give up His spirit after an unheard-of three hours on the cross....most people took days to slowly die on the Roman execution device.

But He didn't stay on the cross!

Blessed assurance, *He didn't stay on the cross!*

No, He was taken down when He died and was wrapped in burial cloths with myrrh and frankincense — common embalming elements then — and placed in a borrowed tomb. A heavy stone was rolled into place, a Roman seal and guard were placed, and the world waited.

All of heaven waited.

For three days, as the disciples huddled in fear for their own lives and satan and his demons cheered in apparent victory, it seemed like Jesus had failed. It seemed like Jesus' dead body was in the tomb for good.

But — *He didn't stay in that tomb!*

That stone was rolled away not for Jesus to get out — No! But for His disciples and for the world and for satan to look in — in to a very echoing, hollow, empty tomb.

The tomb was empty! Jesus didn't stay in the tomb....and He made His bed! Now, in ancient Jewish culture, when the man of the house was going to come back to the meal, was just taking a break from eating, he would fold his napkin — a sign to the servants to wait, that he would be back — don't be hasty and remove his plate. If the man wadded his napkin and placed it on his plate, that signaled he was not coming back.

Look at these words, study them: *Jesus folded his napkin.*

For forty days after the Resurrection, Jesus taught His disciples. Certainly they paid a lot more attention this time around. Then, with his disciples following, Jesus walked up the Mount of Olives, told them to go, share, teach....

He didn't stay on the mountain. He didn't stay on this earth.

He ascended to the throne of God, where He sat down at the right hand of God the Father. *But He's not going to stay there.*

He's coming back, friends.

Jesus is coming back.

For Reflection:

Just as people waited anxiously for the Messiah to be born, we wait anxiously for Jesus the Victor to return for His Bride, the Church. This Reflection is simple: When Jesus returns for His followers in the Rapture, will you go...or will you stay?

How can you share the Good News of Jesus atoning sacrifice to your loved ones, and the fact He will come again?

What Gift Will You Bring?

"When they saw the star, they were overjoyed. On coming to the house, they saw the child with his mother Mary, and they bowed down and worshiped him. Then they opened their treasures and presented him with gifts of gold and of incense and of myrrh." Matthew 2:10-11

The wise men from the east brought expensive gifts to the Christ Child, treasures that Joseph and Mary probably never dreamed they'd see in their lifetimes. Their gifts were highly symbolic of the Babe that lay before them.

Gold – a gift for a king, symbolizing His Kingship. Revelation 19:16 states that Jesus is indeed King: "On his robe and on his thigh he has this name written: KING OF KINGS AND LORD OF LORDS." Jesus came to this earth a peasant baby, as low on the society totem pole as one could possibly be; yet, this Child will return one day to collect His own and rule over the earth that is His.

Incense – a fragrant gift, designed to be used by the High Priest to waft to the throne room of God. This symbolizes Christ as our High Priest. He came as the High Priest and the sacrifice, to give once and for all. "When Christ came as high priest of the good things that are already here, he went through the greater and more perfect tabernacle that is not man-made, that is to say, not a part of this creation. He did not enter by means of the blood of goats and calves; but he entered the Most Holy Place once for all by his own blood, having obtained eternal redemption," Hebrews 9: 11-12.

Lastly, the gift of myrrh…designed to be used to anoint the bodies of the dead for burial. This gift – which surely must have caused Mary to catch her breath – symbolizes Christ's sacrifice. His entire birth was overshadowed by the cross; indeed, it is why God sent Him. "For God so loved the world that he gave his one and only Son, that whoever believes in him shall not perish but have eternal life," John 3:16.

The wise men came prepared to meet Christ, armed with gifts of extraordinary value. This Christmas, as baubles and trinkets are wrapped and under the tree for loved ones, think about the Gift you will give Christ this Christmas. He has already given us a gift – Himself, the greatest Gift – on His own birthday. How then shall we honor His birthday? Shall we spend more time in fellowship with Him through reading His Word and prayer? Increase our tithe? Consider ways we may serve Him through mission work, donating to missionaries, or even mentoring a child? Sharing His Good News with loved ones – and those we don't love so much? Living the life God intended for us to live, one of Christ-centered-ness, where Christmas exists in our hearts 365 days of the year instead of when the stores say it does?

For Reflection:

What gift will you bring to the manger?

Is There Room in Your Inn?

"While they were there, the time came for the baby to be born, and she gave birth to her firstborn, a son. She wrapped him in cloths and placed him in a manger, because there was no room for them in the inn." Luke 2:6-7

What is Christmas about to you? Is it about the presents under the tree? Getting together with family and friends? With all the hub-bub, glitz and stuff of Christmastime, is there room in your heart for the Christ of Christmas?

It is easy in this day and age to get swept up in the whirlwind that exists after October 31, through the month of November, hiccupping just enough at Thanksgiving to catch our breath, swallow a lot of nourishment just to have energy to fight crowds on Black Friday. Scripture says to "Be still, and know that I am God," [Psalm 46:10]. Is there room on the yuletide to-do list for sitting still?

Joseph and Mary traveled what scholars think

was a 90-mile journey on donkeyback, heavy laden with the impending pregnancy, just to have a "no vacancy" sign shoved in their face. Yet, Mary in her faithfulness brought "swaddling cloths" to wrap the newborn King of Kings in. This can be a profound lesson to us all. In our frenzied Christmastime, let us too prepare our hearts and minds to meet the Christ-Child this season. Let us open our hearts, minds and souls to the Jesus this December and experience a richer, more fulfilling Christmas than ever before.

Jesus said, "Here I am! I stand at the door and knock. If anyone hears my voice and opens the door, I will come in and eat with him, and he with me" [Revelation 3:20]. This December, when Jesus stands knocking at the door of your Inn, will you open the door and let Him in, or tell Him there is no room?

For Reflection…

What are your favorite memories of Christmas past? What made them special?

How can we prepare our hearts to welcome Jesus this Christmas?

Wrapped in Cloth

"While they were there, the time came for the baby to be born, and she gave birth to her firstborn, a son. She wrapped him in cloths and placed him in a manger, because there was no guest room available for them." [Luke 2:6-7].

I bathed my eight-month old baby girl, Laura. She had recently learned how to splash the water; the joy on her face as she did that made me smile as I held onto her with one hand and bathed her with the other. As I put the pocket of the infant towel over her head and picked her up, wrapping the towel around her, she was shivering; six new wee little teeth chattered as she looked at me with wide brown eyes imploring me to hurry and get her dressed.

As I dressed her for bed, I was reminded that Mary also dressed Baby Jesus. He was born, and then ever so gently, His mother wrapped Him with clothes, to keep Him warm, to protect Him from the elements. This little baby boy had rough and tumble shepherds visit Him after a choir of angels proclaimed His birth — even a star twinkled more powerfully for the occasion. The entire earth bowed when the Baby King Jesus was born.

We sometimes forget, and fast-forward to the times when Jesus was all grown-up, to the times He was dispelling demons into pigs, upturning the tables in the temple, making water into wine, being beaten and tortured and dying for us, then coming back to life three days later.

In the power and awesomeness of Easter, we forget the humility of Christmas.

For God came down to earth not in the form of a man, but in the unexpected fragility of a tiny baby boy. This baby boy, who will one day be called the King of Kings and Lord of Lords and call all who call on Him home to heaven, started out as a delicate infant who napped, nursed, woke up at night, used his thumb for a teething ring, and smiled at the wonder of angels who no doubt smiled back around his bed. This little baby boy is the Wonder of Christmas.

If Mary cared enough to wrap Jesus in clothes and lay him gently in a manger, no doubt filled with fresh straw — how much more should we protect Him? Yes, He promises us He will be with us and never abandon us — but He also says "But whoever disowns me before others, I will disown before my Father in heaven." {Matthew 10:33}.

So then, how do we protect Jesus? We say Merry *Christ*mas, we emphasize Jesus more than Santa, we remember the sacrifice that God made to free us from the bondage of sin through His son, Jesus Christ. We protect this sacrifice by living our lives in such a way that, like the star that twinkled for His birth over Bethlehem, the Light that shines in us can lead others to Christ.

For Reflection...

Think on this: "In the power and awesomeness of Easter, we forget the humility of Christmas." What aspects of Christmas do you think of regarding "humility"?

What aspects of Easter do you think of as being powerful?

Swaddling Cloths:
The Meaning of Preparation

"And she brought forth her firstborn son, and wrapped him in swaddling clothes, and laid him in a manger; because there was no room for them in the inn." ~ Luke 2:7 KJV

This often-quoted Scripture greets us at Christmastime. We like to think of the sweet Baby Jesus resting quietly and comfortably first in his mother's arms, then sleeping peacefully in a manger filled with sweet-smelling hay. This verse though has other meanings that are relevant in other months besides December.

As is usually the case in studying Scripture, the lesson is in the details. When Scripture is very specific in a description, there is a knowledge-nugget to be gleaned. In this verse, the nugget is in the phrase "swaddling clothes."

According to Hebrew history and culture, swaddling cloths were made from linen or cotton material, and were five to six yards long (15-18 feet). The width of the band was four to five inches. Salt was crushed and pulverized by the midwife until it was in the form of a fine powder. When the baby was born, the baby was first washed in water, then a piece of cloth about a square yard in size was laid out and the baby placed on it in a diagonal position. The baby was then wrapped with the bands so that his arms and legs could not flounder about. We swaddle newborns with blankets like this today — it gives them a sense of security.

The Luke passage mentions that Mary delivered Jesus and wrapped Him in swaddling cloths. These swaddling cloths took a long time to make, and it would have been up to Mary to make them. Like expecting moms who go to the department store and put baby items on registry lists, Mary must have thought about her baby with every turn of the loom while making the bands. She prepared herself while preparing the bands, thinking about the way in which He was conceived, wondering what The Lord God had in store for the baby -- and her. She was humbled and amazed God would choose her to be on this journey with Him. She was preparing to meet her Son — and her Savior.

A couple of years ago, I was preparing to travel to Zambia, Africa on a mission trip. While shopping for games for the orphaned children there, and clothing, toiletries, etc, I remembered this passage and the preparation of the swaddling cloths. Not that I was preparing to meet Jesus, for I knew He is with me, but in preparing for the trip, I had the sense that Jesus was preparing me to witness a mighty work He would do — in the orphanage, in the mission team, in the bush pastors we were going to train. To be involved in just the preparations was exciting.

When I was editing a nonprofit newsletter, I would write and edit the articles, outline which articles, ads, photos and graphics would go on each page, then methodically design the newsletter using the outline I made. It made preparing the newsletter a consistent process, and eliminated (most) of the stress involved in a monthly publication. The Bible is our "outline" for preparing to meet God in His work — whether that is a mission trip, a community care day, a building campaign or teaching a Sunday School class.

"In a large house there are articles not only of gold and silver, but also of wood and clay; some are for special purposes and some for common use. Those who cleanse themselves from the latter will be instruments for special purposes, made holy, useful to the Master and prepared to do any good work." [2 Timothy 2:20-21].

Once we prepare to do God's work, all jobs take on special meaning, as unto the Lord. From teaching or leading a Bible study, to preaching — to taking out the trash and changing baby diapers, all should be done in Jesus' name. 1st Corinthians 10:31 states, "So whether you eat or drink or whatever you do, do it all for the glory of God."

Once we put down our own egos, that's when God can *really* use us. It's through His strength and power, not our's, to do His work. For if it was in our strength, where would the glory be for Him? He gives the strength and it's for His glory, not our's. "If anyone speaks, they should do so as one who speaks the very words of God. If anyone serves, they should do so with the strength God provides, so that in all things God may be praised through Jesus Christ. To Him be the glory and the power for ever and ever. Amen." [1st Peter 4:11].

Even as I was wrapping up a final fundraising push, and finalizing packing lists so I didn't leave anything (and certainly not go over airline baggage weight limits), it was at the forefront of my mind that God was preparing a great harvest. "For we are God's handiwork, created in Christ Jesus to do good works, which God prepared in advance for us to do." [Ephesians 2:10]

How humbling it is that He has called us to share in His work! The Ephesians passage is remarkable to me — that before I even accepted Christ as Savior, He had prepared the African mission trip for me and the other team members at church.

We are created in Jesus to do His good works, which God Himself prepared and outlined for us to do in and through Him. We are all commanded to fulfill His great commission — to go into all the world, sharing His gospel, and teaching others about Him. To me, it is incredible that the God of the Universe, who sets the earth on its axis and paints sunsets with a silent word, would whisper my name and the word "Africa." *Wow*. That makes me love Him more.

For Reflection:

What has God been leading you to do? Go on a mission trip? Witness to that co-worker?

What have been your reasons not to do these things?

Right now, pray and ask God to remove these reasons…and thank Him that He would include you in His plan.

A Voice is Heard in Ramah

"When they had gone, an angel of the Lord appeared to Joseph in a dream "Get up," he said, "take the child and his mother and escape to Egypt. Stay there until I tell you, for Herod is going to search for the child to kill him." So he got up, took the child and his mother during the night and left for Egypt, where he stayed until the death of Herod. And so was fulfilled what the Lord had said through the prophet: "Out of Egypt I called my son."

When Herod realized that he had been outwitted by the Magi, he was furious, and he gave orders to kill all the boys in Bethlehem and its vicinity who were two years old and under, in accordance with the time he had learned from the Magi. Then what was said through the prophet Jeremiah was fulfilled:

"A voice is heard in Ramah,
weeping and great mourning,
Rachel weeping for her children

and refusing to be comforted,
because they are no more."
~ Matthew 2:13-18

There are parts of the Christmas story that leave more questions than answers. Some parts have been omitted by the Author and keep us guessing, like how long was Mary's labor? Did Joseph smack the King of Kings and Lord of Lords on His bottom to get Him to cry and therefore breathe His first human breath – and did *Joseph hesitate to do that?* Wouldn't *you* hesitate to smack God's bottom? And there are other questions, too. Did the Baby wrap His tiny fingers around His mother's pinky finger as He nursed? Did He have colic?

One question that is answered in five verses is this: there were people who, even then, tried to take the Christ out of Christmas. Herod was so filled with jealousy and rage he demanded all baby boys two years and younger to be murdered – murdered in their mother's arms, slaughtered as they crawled on dirt floors, killed in their beds. We tend to skip over this part of the Christmas story – the Wise Men go their way, and Joseph relocates the family to Egypt. One would think he had been transferred without much fanfare, if carpenters back then were transferred every day.

God sent an angel to Joseph in a dream, a dream that most certainly woke him up, panic-filled, drenched in sweat and crying. A dream that made him sit straight up in bed and look at his sleeping wife beside him cradling the Baby. The Baby's brown eyes were wide open and staring at Joseph, as though they were saying: *"You know what you must do."* A dream that caused Joseph's heart to skip a beat and start to panic as he shook Mary awake. "Wake up! Wake up! We must leave! Don't take anything – just pick up Jesus – I'll get the donkey!"

Most certainly as Joseph threw a blanket over the donkey, he heard them: gut-wrenching, terrified, soul-crushing screams. Coming from everywhere. Soldiers kicking in doors and mothers wailing as Joseph ran with the donkey, struggling under the weight of Mary and the Baby, running in the shadows, afraid to even breathe. Mary sobbing – she knew what was happening, knew they were looking for Him, knew her friends were having their boys killed without mercy in their very arms. Mary clung to her Lord, her Child, her precious little Baby, her whole body heaving with quiet sobs.

That Baby – as much as the donkey was jiggling them and bouncing them, any other time He would be crying. Not tonight. He was wide-eyed, but not crying – He knew better. He was also mesmerized, looking up at the mobile of bright angels that were swirling around the three of them, with an archangel in front of the very focused donkey, sword drawn. These angels would not let the soldiers' knives and spears come near this Child.

They made it to Egypt, running for nights and days, running from the throng of soldiers that were on a death-march all over Herod's jurisdiction. But despite all the funerals that went on for days and days, Herod's jealous rage was not successful in stopping God's purpose for the Christ-Child. He came out of Egypt years later, even as Moses did with the Hebrews, fulfilling prophecy, the One and Only Male of His age from that province to survive that awful, terrible night.

Herod did not succeed in taking the Christ out of Christmas. May God be with us all as we celebrate the Christ in Christmas and the real reason for the season – it's not having a naughty-or-nice checklist, it's not about having the perfect decorations, it's not about giving or receiving or clinking quarters in kettles...it's about a little Baby, born of God and Mary, raised by a loving, God-filled foster father, to come into the world to die for us, to be raised from the dead for us, to be with us even now – He was Immanuel, *God with us*, two thousand years ago; He is Immanuel today. Praise be to God.

For Reflection:

How can you keep Christ in Christmas in your home? Workplace?

How can you shine the light of Christ in traffic, or in busy stores, or in waiting rooms? The Light of Christ is not supposed to just be for Sundays.

Better than Stable-Born

Often when my boys were younger and they'd leave the front door open, I say to them, "Shut the door! Only Jesus was born in a barn!" But I couldn't have been more wrong.

Sometimes the Christmas story is hard to understand — what righteous, very Jewish parents would even want to give birth in a very unclean, smelly stable or barn? Here's the thing: Jesus being born in a manger was so much bigger than just a circumstance of not finding a hotel room.

It was a prophecy come true. It had everything to do with His death.

In order to understand this, we must look in the Old Testament at the numerous animal, particularly lamb, sacrifices. We must not only study the Bible but also look at ancient Hebrew culture and tradition — for in Jewish history, tradition and religion are inseparable...and this, thankfully, helps the modern day biblical scholar understand points in Scripture, thanks be to God.

First, let's examine two passages in Micah, 5:2 and 4:8:

"But you, Bethlehem Ephrathah,
though you are small among the clans of Judah,
out of you will come for me
one who will be ruler over Israel,
whose origins are from of old,
from ancient times." ~ Micah 5:2

"As for you, watchtower of the flock,
stronghold of Daughter Zion,
the former dominion will be restored to you;
kingship will come to Daughter Jerusalem."   ~ Micah 4:8

We know from Micah 5:2 that Jesus would be born in Bethlehem. In ancient Hebrew tradition and history, Bethlehem was a central location for shepherds who kept flocks of sheep. Located about four miles from Jerusalem and the temple where animal sacrifices were a daily occurrence, the shepherds had to keep an astronomical amount of sheep for the sacrifices.

Because of the magnitude of sheep needed, they could not be housed indoors. They were pastured outside. Ezekiel 46:13 states, "'Every day you are to provide a year-old lamb without defect for a burnt offering to the Lord; morning by morning you shall provide it." That's 365 lambs a year. That's a flock in itself!

But now read Numbers 29. That is a huge amount of sheep! Perfect, unblemished sheep. It would take someone acquainted with religious rites and temple requirements to make sure the lambs brought to the altar were, in a word, kosher. That is why the shepherds that guarded the flocks by night were not ragamuffin shepherds but temple shepherds. According to Hebrew culture, temple shepherds specifically trained for this task. They knew what to look for in the lambs: No blemishes. Nothing physically wrong with them. Many needed to be male, but some female lambs were used (see Leviticus 4:32 and 5:6).
Micah 4:8 talks about this intriguing phrase, "watchtower of the flock." This tall stone building was where the shepherds could keep a watchful eye over the large flock as they grazed nearby. The bottom of the watchtower, called *Migdal*

Eder in Hebrew, afforded the shepherds a safe place in which to take care of pregnant ewes.

Because it was of utmost importance that the lambs remain holy to the Lord, it was crucial that where the perfect lambs were born in an environment that was not unclean, safe, and not around filth as in a common stable. In biblical times, barns or stables were used to store grains, produce, etc — not animals, especially sheep (see Proverbs 3:10; Haggai 2:19; Matthew 3:12, 6:26, 13:30; Luke 3:17, 12:18; 12:24 and Psalm 144:13).

The bottom of the Migdal Eder, was where the pregnant ewes were taken to safely and cleanly birth the perfect, unblemished lambs for temple sacrifice. This room at the base of the Migdal Eder was called a *manger*.

I've got goosebumps all over just writing that. God didn't haphazardly send His Son down to the earth. Every part of His sending was part of the plan of salvation. Think about it: Mary is in labor pains, Joseph in his panic after knocking on inn doors, looks out, sees the tall tower of Migdal Eder, knows about the manger, knows that it would be clean and safe. He takes Mary there, sees that the shepherds are not there but are out in the fields, and gently helps Mary down among the hay and straw.

"While they were there, the time came for the baby to be born, and she gave birth to her firstborn, a son. She wrapped him in cloths and placed him in a manger, because there was no guest room available for them," Luke 2:6-7.

Think about this. The Lamb of God, born of a virgin, in a manger — in a manger where the sacrificial lambs of God destined for the altar are born.

Goosebumps.

Then, out in the fields — Gabriel, who could barely contain himself, appears to the shepherds. "But the angel said to them, "Do not be afraid. I bring you good news that will cause great joy for all the people. Today in the town of David a Savior has been born to you; He is the Messiah, the Lord. This will be a sign to you: You will find a baby wrapped in cloths and lying in a manger," Luke 2:10-12.

Notice Gabriel did not give them further directions. He only said "town of David" and "manger." You can almost see the shepherds look at one another and say, "We just came from there!" They didn't need any other directions because they knew what the angel was talking about when he said "manger."

Then, in the first ever Hallelujah Chorus, "Suddenly a great company of the heavenly host appeared with the angel, praising God and saying, "Glory to God in the highest heaven, and on earth peace to those on whom his favor rests," Luke 2:13-14. *Poof!* The angels were gone, leaving darkness swallowing up the shepherds, who immediately ran to the manger.

Centuries before this, Abraham, leading Isaac up the mountain to be sacrificed in an act of obedience, told his boy, "...God himself will provide the lamb for the burnt offering, my son." And the two of them went on together," Genesis 22:8.

Indeed, God sent His only Son to be, like the story of Isaac, a substitution for us, being born to die so that we may be reborn and live. Every aspect of Christ's birth, life and death is rich in detail and meaning. The word "manger" has been translated and changed over 2,000 years to mean a place where wheat is put for cattle, but even that has meaning — the Bread of Life....

There are many explanations behind the manger — born in a cave, because that's where animals were kept, and the cave was like a tomb, etc. But I think God in His attention to detail would provide more for His Son and the young couple He chose and invited on this journey. The thought that God would send His Son to be born, live, die and — Praise God! — *live again*! makes me want to pull a Gabriel and shout it!

For Reflection:

God provided the elements of Jesus' sacrifice long before it happened. What does this say to you about His provision for you?

Think about the sights, sounds and – yes, smells – of the manger. Think about Mary's first impression about delivering there. What would have been your thoughts?

Sources:

"Migdal Eder" by Rabbi Mike L. Short.
http://www.mayimhayim.org/Rabbi%20Mike/Migdal%20Eder.htm

"Shepherds: More Than Field Hands" by Dr. Charlie Dyer, host of "The Land and the Book." http://www.moodyradio.org/uploadedFiles/Broadcasting/Specials/Dyer_Blog_ShepherdsMoreThanFieldHands.pdf?n=5478

"The Tower of the Flock" by Dr. Juergen Buehler. http://int.icej.org/news/commentary/tower-flock

Songs of Praise

Angels take on a special place at Christmas. There are simple angels, ornate celestial beings, chubby cherubs, with a wide variety between these standards.

In the Bible, angels were given very specific jobs. Gabriel announced to Zachariah that he was to have a son that would be the forerunner of the Christ, who would actually be his cousin. Gabriel also delivered a baby announcement to young Mary. It's interesting to note that both times Gabriel told the recipient of the good news, "Do not be afraid." Since seeing angels was not an everyday occurrence, it's easy to see how the first words out of their mouths were of reassurance.

The primary purposes of angels are to praise God and to serve Him. "In the sixth month, God sent the angel Gabriel to Nazareth, a town in Galilee, to a virgin pledged to be married to a man named

Joseph, a descendant of David." (Luke 1:26-27).
God *sent* Gabriel to Mary, to tell her she, a young
girl, was going to be the Messiah's mother. Soon
after this, an unnamed angel appeared to Joseph
in a dream and told him to not be afraid – but this
time, it was reassurance to not be afraid to take
Mary as his wife. Perhaps Joseph's fear about
Mary was greater than seeing an angel in his
sleep.

An angel also appeared to shepherds, keeping
their flocks by night, in the pastures around
Bethlehem. This angel, perhaps Gabriel,
announced to this group of shepherds that the
long-awaited Messiah, Immanuel, the Christ, was
born. Suddenly, as though their joy could be
contained no longer, an entire choir of heavenly
host burst onto the scene. Such a birth
announcement could only mean one thing: the
Son of God had been born. The angels cried out,
"Glory to God in the highest, and on earth peace
to men on whom his favor rests." (Luke 2:14)

This announcement holds great promise for us.
While its main focus is glorifying God, as well as
it should, the angelic choir also announced the
birth of the Prince of Peace. "Therefore, since we
have been justified through faith, we have peace

with God through our Lord Jesus Christ..."
(Romans 5:1). Isaiah 9:6 states, "For to us a child
is born, to us a son is given, and the government
will be on his shoulders. And he will be called
Wonderful Counselor, Mighty God, Everlasting
Father, Prince of Peace."

In the future, the choir of angels will again burst
into song, as Revelation 5:11-13 joyously
proclaims. "Then I looked and heard the voice of
many angels, numbering thousands upon
thousands, and ten thousand times ten thousand.
They encircled the throne and the living creatures
and the elders. In a loud voice they sang:

"Worthy is the Lamb, who was slain,
to receive power and wealth and wisdom and
strength
and honor and glory and praise!"

The choir of angels had shout-sung a Holy birth
announcement to a bunch of shepherds. In the
future, the choir will crown with jubilee the King
of Kings, the Lamb of God. But they will not be
alone, as every knee will bow and every mouth
will sing:

"Then I heard every creature in heaven and on earth and under the earth and on the sea, and all that is in them, singing:

"To him who sits on the throne and to the Lamb be praise and honor and glory and power, forever and ever!" ~ Revelation 5:13

This Christmas, may we join with the angels in singing praises to God and His Son. May we be filled with joy, not about the stockings hung with care or of a new bicycle or a new bathrobe, but of Immanuel – God with us. May we remember, with joy, that God sent His only Son, serenaded by angels, because He loved us so.

For Reflection:

For what can you praise Jesus right this minute?

Plot and Setting

We read books or watch movies and take note of the plot and setting. The plot twists, and we don't see it coming, and we think the writer is so clever. In real life, though, to see how the plots of our lives work out, usually takes looking at life in hindsight. We can't see while the twists and turns are happening in real time, how God will work out the crisis du jour….but He does.

We read in the Bible (Luke 1:26) that Mary lived in Nazareth, a town in Galilee. When Mary was in her sixth month, she visited relatives Elizabeth and Zachariah in a town in the hill country of Judea. In Biblical times, unlike today, people just didn't go on vacations. A person had to have a reason to travel – visiting family, like Mary did, or for business.

So why in the world would a young, newly married, very pregnant girl travel with her husband to a village eighty miles away, which equals a four-day journey? How could the Old

Testament prophecy be fulfilled, that stated Bethlehem would be the place of the Messiah's birth? "But you, Bethlehem Ephrathah, though you are small among the clans of Judah, out of you will come for me one who will be ruler over Israel, whose origins are from of old, from ancient times." (Micah 5:2)

Isaiah wrote, "For to us a child is born, to us a son is given, and the government will be on his shoulders. And he will be called Wonderful Counselor, Mighty God, Everlasting Father, Prince of Peace" (9:6).

How awesome it is that even before Jesus was born, the government was on his shoulders? "In those days Caesar Augustus issued a decree that a census should be taken of the entire Roman world. (This was the first census that took place while Quirinius was governor of Syria.) And everyone went to his own town to register" (Luke 2:1-2). God placed in the mind of Caesar Augustus to issue a census of the entire Roman world. Joseph, of the house and lineage of David, had to go to David's town of origin, so he and his new bride could be counted in this Roman census. David's town of origin was Bethlehem.

We may sometimes wonder what God is up to in our lives by the twists and turns that life seems to take. Joseph must have thought that the census, with Mary being great with child, must have come at a most unfortunate time. No, Joseph, it came on God's time, bringing to life the Scripture of Jeremiah 29:11: "For I know the plans I have for you," declares the LORD, "plans to prosper you and not to harm you, plans to give you hope and a future."

For Reflection:

Name an instance in your life when something happened at a most busy and unfortunate time.

How did God intervene?

The Light of the World

While on a mission trip to Africa, I was amazed at the stars. In the United States, there is so much light pollution that one cannot fully appreciate the incredible beauty and power of the star-filled sky.

The first night in Zambia, I was overcome with the Holy Spirit and had to go outside to gaze upon the stars, the Milky Way, the galaxies swirling above. The suffocating darkness around me on the ground was impenetrable; I was certain a lion was marking me for a target, lurking in the darkness. But all that did not matter; I was surrounded inside and out with the Holy Spirit, kneeling on a towel and praying Psalm 8 to the Lord God:

"LORD, our Lord,
  how majestic is your name in all the earth!
You have set your glory in the heavens.
Through the praise of children and infants
you have established a stronghold against your

enemies, to silence the foe and the avenger.
When I consider your heavens,
the work of your fingers,
the moon and the stars,
which you have set in place,
what is mankind that you are mindful of them,
human beings that you care for them?[c]
You have made them[d] *a little lower than the*
angels[e]
and crowned them[f] *with glory and honor.*
You made them rulers over the works of your
hands;
you put everything under their feet:
all flocks and herds,
and the animals of the wild,
the birds in the sky,
and the fish in the sea,
all that swim the paths of the seas.
LORD, our Lord,
how majestic is your name in all the earth!"

About two thousand years ago, the stars burst forth, shining like Christmas lights for the entire world to see. They were shining to mark where the Light of the World was born. Inanimate, balls of gas, the stars shone over Jesus' house where

He lived in Bethlehem after He was born, a lighthouse for the visiting Magi.

It's amazing that the stars shone over His house. When my daughter was born we hung a pink wreath on the door; some people put giant plywood storks in their yards announcing a special delivery has been made. God the Creator of the Universe, Who sent His only Son to earth as a Baby, went all-out to announce that Jesus, the Light of the world, was here.

God told us He would do this, though. "And God said, "Let there be lights in the vault of the sky to separate the day from the night, and let them serve as signs to mark sacred times, and days and years," [Genesis 1:14]. Those lights came out at His birth – certainly a sacred, quiet, humble time. Other than the angels' glorious baby announcement that shocked shepherds, the star was the only other sign that marked His birth.

It's not the only time though that God's creation stood on guard to worship their Creator. When Jesus was riding into Jerusalem on a donkey's back, with worshippers all around throwing coats and fig leaves on the ground in front of him, Jesus shared a praise report with a local naysayer:

"When he came near the place where the road goes down the Mount of Olives, the whole crowd of disciples began joyfully to praise God in loud voices for all the miracles they had seen:

"Blessed is the king who comes in the name of the Lord!"
"Peace in heaven and glory in the highest!"
Some of the Pharisees in the crowd said to Jesus, "Teacher, rebuke your disciples!"

"I tell you," he replied, "if they keep quiet, *the stones will cry out*."[Luke 19:37-40, emphasis added].

If the people didn't cry out, the stones would cry out! From dancing stars to praising stones, all of creation bows to the King! As He died on the cross, the sky darkened at noontime – something never seen before – and thunder rolled across the sky. All of nature was expressing God's feelings as His Only Begotten Son gave up the Spirit.

Biblical scholars believe that the Magi's journey was about two years long as they followed the star. Thinking that King Herod would certainly know where this Royal Child was born, they went to him first. "After Jesus was born in Bethlehem in Judea, during the time of King Herod, Magi from the east came to Jerusalem and asked, "Where is the one who has been born king of the Jews? We saw his star when it rose and have come to worship him," [Matthew 2:1-2].

This angered King Herod and frightened him. How dare a usurping Boy-King be born in his vicinity and he not know it! Yet John wrote of this in John 1:9-11: "The true light that gives light to everyone was coming into the world. He was in the world, and though the world was made through him, the world did not recognize him. He came to that which was his own, but his own did not receive him."

One can be so close to Jesus yet not know Him.

The Magi found out that Bethlehem was where they needed to go, so they headed out to this suburb of Jerusalem, finding the star hovering over the very house. They walked in, offering gifts fit for royalty, and knelt at the Toddler Jesus, who was about two years old at the time.

One wonders if Jesus knew, at two years old, what was happening, or if He in His Godly power suppressed His knowledge enough to be a toddler; after all, He was all-God *and* all-man. I wonder if He played with the gold coins, or wanted to put the myrrh in His mouth. I wonder if He hid behind His mother's skirt and peeked out at these strange-looking men kneeling before Him. I wonder if He warmed up to them and held His arms up to be picked up.

The wonder of it: the Light of the world, being picked up and held by an earthly king who had searched and found Him. I wonder if He pulled the Magi's beard.

I wonder if He giggled when the Magi tickled Him, or ran to Joseph coming in the door, amazed at the men standing in his home.

John 1:14 states, "The Word became flesh and made his dwelling among us. We have seen his glory, the glory of the one and only Son, who came from the Father, full of grace and truth." A brilliant star shining brightly, leading Magi to Jesus, dulls in comparison to God's glory, Who is Jesus.

The brilliant star led wise men to Jesus, the Light of the World. How much more should we shine to lead others to Him.

Compare the Magi's request (verse 2) to worship Jesus with Herod's (verse 8). The Magi have *come* to worship; Herod wanted to *go* and worship. What is the difference between coming to worship Christ and going to do so? [Hint: it's a heart thing].

What other times in the Bible did God use His creation to do His will?

Out of Egypt

God has a way of bringing Scripture home to us. The Holy Spirit makes oft-read passages come alive as though we've never read them before. Truly, "For the word of God is alive and active. Sharper than any double-edged sword, it penetrates even to dividing soul and spirit, joints and marrow; it judges the thoughts and attitudes of the heart," [Hebrews 3:12].

The mission trip to Africa in 2013 had a profound effect on me. Honestly, I cannot wait to go back. We stayed on a farm near the village where we served, and utilized an open-air hut as a gathering place for the team to have breakfast, meals with area pastors and their wives, and a Holy Spirit-drenched foot washing and concert of prayer.

One day, while walking to breakfast to the open-air, thatched hut from the farmhouse, I had the sudden and incredible realization that my feet were walking on African soil – the very same continent that Jesus walked on as a little boy. Goosebumps covered my arms.

Sure, I was hundreds of miles away from Egypt where Jesus was reared as a little boy, but the same continent....for someone who has never been to Israel, knowing that my feet were touching a continent Jesus played tag on or jumped in the Nile for a swim warmed my heart. Oh, precious Lord! God is so good to give us these little glimpses of Himself, even as we walk to breakfast.

The journey to Egypt for Jesus was a hurried one, but still in the mad dash to save the Savior, God provided. He sent an angel to warn Joseph in a dream that Herod was coming to kill Jesus, and to go to Egypt. This also served to fulfill a prophecy: "When Israel was a child, I loved him, and out of Egypt I called my son, [Hosea 11:1].

God has a way of bringing Scripture home to us, to make it more real. One night when I was far along in my pregnancy with my daughter, I was preparing to go to bed and my husband noticed that I was a lot more quiet than usual. I told him that I just did not feel well (I was, after all, eight months pregnant).

After a few minutes of laying down, sitting up, pacing the floor and holding my belly, my husband was pretty well convinced I was going to have the baby any moment. So, despite it being ten o'clock at night, off we went to the hospital. It proved to be a false alarm, but he made sure a bag was packed after that.

During this hurried, late-night trip to the emergency room, I remembered the late-night trip that Mary, Joseph and the Baby launched on, to avoid Herod's soldiers and keep the Child safe. Surely they were scared, tired, and trying to keep it together for each other's sake. When we allow God to have access to every minute of every day, He is able to bring Scripture home to us, to make it more real. He provides so much more in these moments than protection and His presence. He reminds us that He is the Provision.

One wonders how a poor carpenter could afford a middle-of-the-night, sudden move to another country far away. But God provided a way to keep His Son safe, and provided a way for His mother and adoptive father to be safe as well through the generosity of an act of worship in the Magi's gift of gold.

God is so good. He is the Provider and the Provision. The Magi unknowingly provided, through God, the means by which a poor carpenter could save the Savior from an evil, jealous despot.

I could only imagine Joseph, tossing and turning, as the dream went on. Then, waking and wondering how in the world he could afford a trip like that…then, as though the moonlight snuck in and twinkled on the Magi's gifts, Joseph gasped, and thanked God for His Provision.

For reflection:

How has God provided for you … not just at Christmas but all the year through?

Have you thanked God – really thanked Him – for being the Provider and the Provision?

We put the tree up, string lights on it, assemble the nativity on the mantle…and sit back to enjoy the twinkling lights, the quiet, the peace. "Merry Christmas" may pass over our lips as a courtesy to clerks and tellers, passers-by and church members. In the quiet sweetness of Christmas, we imagine the Baby's wee little hands wrapped around His mother's pinky finger. We have no desire to imagine those same sweet chubby baby hands pierced and nailed to a cross.

Christmas is all about Easter.

In the manger, the Baby is not a threat. In the manger, the Baby asks nothing of us except to stop and admire. The Jesus of the cross invites us to lay our sins down, look upon Him, and lose ourselves in Him. The Jesus of the cross is a threat to our sin and shame. The Baby, though, is what we tend to focus on and remember at Christmas.

But it is not Christmas that Jesus told us to remember.

"...The Lord Jesus, on the night he was betrayed, took bread, and when he had given thanks, he broke it and said, "This is my body, which is for you; do this in remembrance of me." In the same way, after supper he took the cup, saying, "This cup is the new covenant in my blood; do this, whenever you drink it, in remembrance of me." ~ 1 Corinthians 11:23b-25

Yes, it is right to celebrate Jesus' birth as a love-gift from God Himself. Even the angels celebrated in an epic, shepherd-jaw dropping Hallelujah Chorus. But we are to remember *why* He came.

He did not come for shopper onslaughts of stores and bargains. He did not come to spread good cheer. He did not come to this earth for us to say "season's greetings" or some other ambiguous politically-correct Jesus-avoiding greeting. He did not come for us to give presents to one another or even to give to charities. Yes, those are all good things, but they are not why Jesus was born.

He came for one reason, and the reason is so horrific that we'd just rather go to another bad Christmas sweater contest or eat fruitcake than to dive deep into Christ's mission here on earth.

His reason for being born was to die.

But it wasn't just a random drive-by crucifixion and it certainly wasn't murder by vengeful Jewish leaders or sadistic Roman soldiers. Murder implies that Jesus did not have a say in His death, that it was just a political mess. Murder implies that He was nothing more than a great teacher, an incredible humanitarian, or a prophet. Murder implies He was not fully God in a body that was fully man.

Christ laid down His life for us. It was not taken from Him. Most people who were crucified took *days* to die, as the cross was designed to be a lingering, calculated, tortured death – one that would inspire fear and keep the Jewish people in line. Jesus took three *hours* to die, which was in itself a miracle. He decided when His sacrifice was finished. He decided when to breathe out the Spirit and therefore to give His life as a ransom for us.

But why? Why did this little Baby come to have a death like that?

For you. For me. For us all. We are all sinners, as Romans 3:23 states, "for all have sinned and fall short of the glory of God," Ever since Adam and Eve decided that God's presence wasn't good enough and they wanted more…they wanted to be like Him…and the first sin occurred, man has been heaping sin upon sin on himself. The only way that humanity could even begin to be in the presence of God was through an intersession – through a sacrifice of God's only Son, a perfect Lamb of God.

"For God so loved the world that he gave his one and only Son, that whoever believes in him shall not perish but have eternal life," ~ John 3:16. God did not just give His Son at the cross, but in the cradle, in Bethlehem.

God did not just send Christ down to earth as a grown man, but as a Baby – a helpless, tiny Baby – so that He could experience life here on earth. He relates to us on every conceivable level. Children are special to Him because He was a Child. He knows what it is to laugh, to have friends, to be betrayed. He knows sorrow.

He knows pain.

He longs for us to have an Easter relationship with Him in the joy of Christmas. He wants us to know beyond a shadow of a doubt that in the wonder of Christmas is the dark of Maundy Thursday and the victory – praise Him! Glory! – The *victory* of Easter morning!

For He was not born just to die for us, but He also was born to die to *live again* so that we, in Him and Him alone, might live again with Him.

The majesty of Easter is tucked away among the wonder and quiet peace of Christmas. We celebrate Christmas and Easter – and truly, each day – because of what Christ did. Without Him, life is meaningless. Life is a box, covered in beautiful wrapping paper, but absolutely empty without a relationship with Jesus.

With Jesus, life began in a humble manger...but for us, through Christ, life begins in an empty tomb.

Jesus was born in the shadow of the cross. Everything about His birth, from where He was born to the gifts the wise men bestowed on Him, to the herald angels singing Glory to the Newborn King...everything was about the Reason He came.

That reason, simply, was *us*.

For reflection:

Do you have a relationship with Jesus? Have you asked forgiveness of your sins? Have you repented, or turned away from them, forever turning your back on the old sinful lifestyle you were living in? Have you declared Jesus to be Lord of all, including your life?

If not, and if you want to, please pray this simple prayer, and find a Bible-believing, Word-preaching church pastor to help you understand what this means.

Dear Jesus, I acknowledge you as the Son of God, Who was born, lived and died to take away my sins. I acknowledge to You that I am a sinner, and Jesus, I ask you now to forgive me. I repent of my sins, oh Lord, too numerous to say. I ask You to help me to turn my back on that wicked lifestyle and to proclaim You Lord over my life. Today I become a child of the Risen King, oh Lord, Your child. Thank you. In Jesus' name I pray. Amen.

Friend, welcome to the family of God.

Merry Christmas

Made in United States
North Haven, CT
03 November 2021